Paul Gayler is executive chef at The Lanesborough in London, one of the most fabulous destination hotels in the world. He has worked in some of London's most prestigious restaurants, including The Dorchester and Inigo Jones. Paul has appeared on BBC2's *Saturday Kitchen* and Radio 4's *VegTalk*, as well as being a judge on ITV's *Chef of the Year*. His previous books for Kyle Cathie have been translated into 10 languages and sold 500,000 copies worldwide.

Paul Gayler's **little book of**
ice creams
& sorbets

Paul Gayler's **little book of**

ice cream
& sorbets

sumptuous, mouth-watering, refreshing

Kyle Cathie Limited

For the New Age foodies who demand quality, taste and innovation.

First published in Great Britain in 2009 by
Kyle Cathie Limited
122 Arlington Road
London NW1 7HP
www.kylecathie.com

ISBN 978 1 85626 843 1

Text © 2009 Paul Gayler

Edited by Barbara Bonser
Designed by Mark Jonathan Latter @ Pink Stripe Design
New photography by Will Heap
Styling for new photography by Sheiko and Silvana Franco
Other photographs by Gus Filgate, Steve Lee, Steve Baxter, Richard Jung and Georgia Glynn Smith

Paul Gayler is hereby identified as the author of this work in accordance with Section 77 of the Copyright, Designs and Patents Act 1988.

A Cataloguing in Publication record for this title is available from the British Library.

contents

introduction 6

ice creams 8

sorbets 34

other frozen desserts 62

sauces & accompanying
    dishes 82

index 112

introduction

Once you've tasted home-made ice cream or sorbet, nothing else will do: you simply can't beat the freshness of the flavour. It is an excellent way of using up excess soft fruits during the summer months. Making ice creams and sorbets is about as much fun and rewarding as cooking can get.

It is believed ice creams originated in China as long ago as 3000BC. As contact with the east developed, the secret of making ice cream spread rapidly to Europe. The Romans prepared water ices, and various iced sweets and ice cream methods spread from Italy to France around the 16th century. By the reign of Charles I, ices were extremely fashionable and a delicacy at the English Court. By the 19th century, ice-cream eating had become widespread: ices were sold from booths on street corners in small glass dishes. After ice cream was introduced to America, the ice cream parlour was invented, where it soon began to be commercially produced on a large scale.

Before the invention of the freezer, ice-cream making was a lengthy and tedious process. The cream-based mixture was first placed in a metal bowl which was in turn placed inside a wooden churn lined with crushed ice and salt. The churn was turned with a paddle by hand to prevent the cream crystallising as it froze. When finished, the ice cream was stored in a box, thickly lined with salted ice. Despite these difficulties, chefs and cooks from all over Europe tried to produce more and more elaborate confections, making ice cream bombes by freezing layers of various flavours inside decorative moulds.

History does not seem to record the origin of the sorbet or *granita* (fruit ice) but it is believed it takes its origin from the Persian sharbet or sherbet. Over the centuries these have developed beyond recognition in Italian and French cuisine. Sorbets are much lighter, fresher ices than ice creams; they are based mainly on sugar syrups (sometimes with the addition of egg whites to add lightness).

A good sorbet gets its creaminess by constant churning in an ice-cream machine or whisking occasionally while freezing. Opinions differ about the correct consistency of a sorbet. In former times it was served so soft as to be almost liquid and drinkable. Nowadays it is thought it should be firm enough to scoop into a ball. In Italy, a *granita* is a water ice made in a similar way which has a grainy texture of ice shards deliberately preserved.

ice-cream machines

Serious ice cream makers should invest in an ice-cream machine or sorbetière. These machines have made ice cream and sorbet making far simpler and you can buy some good makes now at reasonable prices. Ice-cream machines vary considerably; it is best to follow the manufacturer's operating instructions at all times for the best results. If you don't own a machine I urge you to invest, they really do make such a difference to the finished product.

hand-beaten method

It is possible to make successful ice creams and sorbets without using a sorbetière by using the freezer, but ice cream made this way freezes harder than that made using the electric churn of the machine. It is difficult to get the satiny smooth finish, as the mixture is not beaten as it freezes.

In this method it is important to whisk the base mixture one or two times during the freezing process. Start by freezing your ice cream or sorbet base in a suitable freezer-proof bowl or container. When it has frozen round the edges (but not in the middle), take it out and whisk until smooth and mushy. Return to the freezer and refreeze. Repeat the process one more time for better results. It is best to transfer the ice cream or sorbet to the fridge about 30 minutes before you intend to eat it. Sorbets and ice creams will take at least 3–4 hours freezing time. Do not attempt to make large quantities of ice cream or sorbets by this method.

freezing & storing

The faster ice creams and sorbets can be frozen, the better the result. Ice creams eaten within a few hours of being made are wonderfully creamy and smooth. Keeping ice creams and sorbets for long periods does little harm, though it does cause a slight deterioration of the texture.

Once completed it is important to store your preparations in well-sealed plastic freezer containers. I also advise covering them with a sealing of clingfilm or kitchen paper under the lid, which prevents crystallization.

Machine made ice creams and sorbets should be taken from the freezer just before they are needed, those made by hand will need to be removed about 30 minutes earlier to the fridge to allow them to soften slowly.

Enjoy the recipes and good eating! All recipes serve 4.

ice creams

This fragrant, rich and creamy ice cream is to die for.
Always make it with good, plump vanilla pods.

vanilla ice cream

250ml full fat milk
350ml double cream
2 plump, soft vanilla pods
6 egg yolks
100g castor sugar
a pinch of salt

Heat the milk and cream in a pan until almost at boiling point, then remove from the heat. Split the vanilla pods open lengthways and scrape out the seeds. Add seeds and pods to the milk and leave to infuse for 20 minutes.

Beat the egg yolks and sugar together until light and fluffy. Remove the vanilla pods from the milk and gradually whisk the milk into the mixture. Return to the pan, add the salt and cook, stirring constantly, over a low heat until the mixture has thickened enough to coat the back of the spoon (do not let it boil or it will curdle).

Remove from the heat, strain through a fine sieve and cool. Chill in the fridge, then freeze in an ice-cream machine according to the manufacturer's instructions.

variations
Infuse 25g lavender, 1 tablespoon of your favourite herb, or fresh Earl Grey tea-leaves instead of vanilla in the milk. Or add 125g lemon curd, dried breadcrumbs, cooked rice pudding, toasted nuts, crumbled Christmas pudding or whisk 100ml of fruity olive oil into the custard base before freezing.

To achieve a great rich-tasting chocolate ice cream, always use a good quality bittersweet dark chocolate couverture with a minimum of 65–70 per cent cacao solids. I also like to add a little honey to the mix, which I think enriches it further.

rich chocolate
ice cream

250ml full fat milk
350ml double cream
1 tablespoon cocoa powder
175g dark bittersweet
  chocolate couverture,
  chopped in small pieces
5 egg yolks
50g castor sugar
2 tablespoons good-quality
  honey

Heat the milk, cream and cocoa powder in a pan until it almost reaches boiling point. Remove from the heat and stir in the chocolate pieces until melted thoroughly.

Beat the egg yolks and sugar in a bowl until light and fluffy. Whisk the hot chocolate cream mixture gently into the eggs and return it to the pan. Stirring constantly over a low heat, thicken the mixture until it coats the back of a spoon (do not let it boil or it will curdle).

Remove from the heat and stir in the honey until melted. Strain through a fine strainer, then chill thoroughly.

Transfer to an ice-cream machine and freeze according to the manufacturer's instructions. Freeze until required.

PG TIPS
There are some wonderful honeys now available in good stores and delicatessens. Lavender and chestnut are two particular favourites which would work well in this recipe, adding a further flavour dimension.

Here is my play on the all-time after-dinner favourite chocolates, "After Eights". Mint and chocolate have a natural affinity together.

mint chocolate chip ice cream

250ml full fat milk
350ml double cream
1 handful of fresh mint leaves
8 egg yolks
200g castor sugar
green food colouring (optional)
2 tablespoons Crème de Menthe
   liqueur
50g dark couverture chocolate
   (70 per cent minimum cacao solids),
   coarsely chopped or grated

Heat the milk and cream in a pan until almost at boiling point. Add the mint, remove from the heat and leave to infuse for 10–15 minutes. Strain through a fine sieve.

Beat the egg yolks and sugar together in a bowl until light and fluffy.

Whisk the mint cream into the egg mixture. Return to a low heat until the mixture has thickened enough to coat the back of a spoon (do not let it boil or it will curdle).

Remove the mixture from the heat, and leave to cool. When cold, add a drip of green food colouring (dip a cocktail stick into the bottle), if desired, to the cream along with the mint liqueur.

Transfer to an ice-cream machine and churn until almost ready before adding the coarsely grated chocolate (this will keep the pieces whole).

Freeze in a plastic container in the normal manner.

Nutmeg and cloves are used to spice up eggnog, a popular rum-based wintertime drink served over Christmas and New Year. Combined with orange peel, it makes a sensational ice cream.

eggnog & orange peel ice cream

200ml full fat milk
400ml double cream
¼–½ teaspoon freshly
   grated nutmeg
5 cloves
6 egg yolks
150g castor sugar
grated zest of 1 orange
100ml dark rum

Put the milk, cream, grated nutmeg and cloves in a pan and bring to the boil. Remove from the heat and leave to infuse for a few minutes.

In a bowl, whisk the egg yolks, sugar, orange zest and rum together until light and fluffy. Pour in the cream mixture, whisking all the time.

Return to the pan and cook gently, stirring constantly, until the mixture thickens enough to coat the back of the spoon (do not let it boil or it will curdle).

Leave to cool, remove the cloves, then pour into an ice-cream machine and freeze according to the manufacturer's instructions. If you don't have an ice-cream machine, follow the instructions for the hand-beaten method on page 7.

fennel, raisin & saffron ice cream

100g fennel
15g unsalted butter
65g castor sugar
1 tablespoon Marie Brizard (or
  other anise liqueur such as
  Pernod)
50g raisins
4 free-range egg yolks
1 free-range egg
500ml whole milk
125ml double cream
2 pinches of saffron strands
1 star anise

Chop the fennel into small raisin-sized dice. Cook gently with the butter and 25g of the sugar for 8 minutes or until soft. Warm the liqueur, pour it over the raisins and leave for 15 minutes. Add the fennel and set aside.

Whisk the egg yolks, whole egg and the remaining sugar together until the mixture whitens. Put the milk, cream, saffron and star anise in a pan and bring to the boil. Pour on to the egg mixture a little at a time, stirring. Return to a clean pan and cook over a gentle heat, stirring all the time with a wooden spoon, until the mixture is thick enough to coat the back of the spoon. Be careful not to let it boil.

Strain the mixture into a clean bowl, then stir in the fennel mixture. Cool the ice cream quickly by standing the bowl in a larger bowl of iced water and stirring until cold. Churn in an ice-cream maker until the mixture resembles semi-whipped cream, then freeze until firm. If you don't have an ice-cream maker, pour the mixture into a bowl and place in the freezer. After 30 minutes, when the mixture is beginning to set, remove from the freezer and beat with an electric beater or hand blender to disperse any ice crystals, then return it to the freezer. Repeat 2 or 3 times, then leave until the ice cream is set firm.

For an unusual vegetable inspired ice cream, sweetcorn makes a great base. If you prefer you can use the same weight of fresh corn on the cob, de-husked and shucked. However you will need to cook the kernels first and purée them for this recipe.

sweetcorn
ice cream

3 free-range egg yolks
1 free-range egg
150g castor sugar
400ml milk
200ml double cream
175g canned sweetcorn, puréed

Whisk the egg yolks, whole egg and sugar together until pale in colour and doubled in volume. Put the milk and cream in a pan and bring to the boil. Pour a little at a time on to the egg mixture, stirring constantly. Add the puréed sweetcorn and strain through a sieve.

Return the mixture to a clean pan and cook over a low heat, stirring constantly with a wooden spoon, until the mixture thickens enough to coat the back of the spoon. Be careful not to let it boil.

Cool the ice cream quickly by standing the bowl in a larger bowl of iced water and stirring until cold. Churn in an ice-cream maker until the mixture resembles semi-whipped cream, then freeze until firm. If you don't have an ice-cream maker, pour the mixture into a bowl and place in the freezer. After 30 minutes, when the mixture is beginning to set, remove from the freezer and beat well with an electric beater or hand blender to disperse any ice crystals, then return it to the freezer. Repeat this 2 or 3 times, then leave until the ice cream is set firm.

This is my favourite caramel ice cream recipe. It is vital that the caramel is cooked long enough to add the right touch of bitterness to the ice cream. If you undercook the sugar, this doesn't give the development of flavour needed.

caramel
ice cream

250ml full fat milk
2 vanilla pods, split
350ml double cream
250g castor or lump sugar
4 tablespoons water
little pinch of salt
8 egg yolks

Heat the milk, vanilla pods and double cream in a pan until almost at boiling point, then remove from the heat. Leave to infuse for 5 minutes.

Place 200g of the sugar along with the water in a heavy based pan and add a pinch of salt. Heat it gently until it loosens, raise the heat gently and, stirring constantly, cook the sugar to a dark amber colour. Quickly remove from the heat and stir in the cream (beware of the bubbles spitting). Mix well together.

Beat the egg yolks and remaining sugar in a bowl until light and fluffy. Whisk in the caramel cream, then return the mixture to the pan and cook gently until it thickens and coats the back of a spoon (do not let it boil or it will curdle.)

Leave to cool then transfer to an ice cream machine and freeze according to the manufacturer's instructions.

PG TIPS
For a wonderful toffee ice cream, add 50g softened unsalted butter to the cooling caramel cream then leave to cool before freezing as above.

Balsamic vinegar's sweet rich flavour works well in this buttery
cream. Serve it with a citrus fruit salad and passion fruit jelly.

balsamic butter ice cream

165g castor sugar
600ml full fat milk, hot
75g unsalted butter
6 egg yolks
1 teaspoon cornflour
4 tablespoons balsamic vinegar

Put 150g of the sugar in a heavy based pan and heat
gently until melted. Raise the heat and cook, without
stirring, until it becomes golden. Pour on the hot milk,
stir well and boil for 1 minute, then remove from the
heat and set aside. In a separate pan, heat the butter
until it foams up and gives off a nutty fragrance. Quickly
strain it through a sieve into a bowl, cover and set aside.

Whisk together the egg yolks and remaining sugar until
pale and creamy. Whisk in the cornflour. Gradually pour
in the caramelised milk and whisk until smooth. Finally,
whisk in the melted butter and balsamic vinegar and
leave to cool. Place in an ice-cream machine and freeze
according to the manufacturer's instructions.

PG TIPS

Make a citrus salad with segments of 2 pink grapefruit,
2 oranges and 2 blood oranges, saving the juice. Bring
the pulp of 10 passion fruit to a boil with 25g sugar and
4 tablespoons water. Add 125ml citrus juice, 85ml sugar
syrup, 2 tablespoons Cointreau and 3 leaves soaked and
drained gelatine. Refrigerate overnight. Serve jelly topped
with fruit segments, balsamic ice cream, and mint.

Always try to taste your berries before you buy them. The best raspberry ice cream is made during our own summer using home-grown varieties.

raspberry ice cream

300g fresh raspberries hulled and
   washed (frozen are fine)
2 tablespoons icing sugar
250ml full fat milk
350ml double cream
1 vanilla pod, split
5 egg yolks
100g castor sugar
juice of ½ small lemon

Place the raspberries in a bowl, sprinkle over the icing sugar, cover and leave to macerate for about 20 minutes.

Heat the milk and cream in a pan, add the vanilla pod and almost bring to the boil, remove from the heat and leave to infuse for 10 minutes. Beat the egg yolks and sugar together in a bowl until light and fluffy. Remove the vanilla pod from the cream and whisk into the egg mixture.

Return to the pan and cook over a low heat until the mixture thickens enough to coat the back of a spoon (do not let it boil or it will curdle). Remove from the heat and cool thoroughly.

Blitz the berries in a blender, then add to the cold cream along with the lemon juice. Transfer to an ice-cream machine and freeze according to the manufacturer's instructions.

PG TIPS
Replace the raspberries with the same amount of hulled and washed strawberries to make strawberry ice cream.

The black pepper gives this ice cream a subtle spicy flavour. It is particularly good served with marinated orange and grapefruit segments.

black pepper ice cream

9 egg yolks
100g castor sugar
250ml milk
250ml double cream
1 level teaspoon freshly ground black
  pepper

Cream together the egg yolks and half the sugar in a bowl. Put the milk, cream, pepper and remaining sugar in a pan and bring to the boil, then pour it over the egg yolks.

Return the mixture to the pan and cook very gently, stirring constantly, until thickened. Strain through a fine strainer and leave to cool, then pour it into an ice-cream maker and freeze until firm, following the manufacturer's instructions.

PG TIPS
On occasions I have been known to add a tipple or two of peach schnapps or rum to the pepper ice cream base. Some may want to leave the pepper grains in the ice cream, rather than straining them out. Pink peppercorns make an unusual variation.

You may be surprised to see goat's cheese in an ice cream, but it gives it a delicious tanginess. The ice cream makes a wonderful foil for cherries – try it with a warm cherry tart or clafoutis.

goat's cheese
ice cream

500ml milk
125ml double cream
4 egg yolks
1 egg
90g castor sugar
125g mild soft goat's cheese

Bring the milk and double cream to the boil. Whisk the egg yolks, whole egg and sugar together until thick, pale and creamy. Pour the milk and cream slowly on to the eggs, whisking all the time. Return the mixture to the pan and stir with a wooden spoon over a gentle heat until it has thickened enough to coat the back of the spoon. Do not let it boil or the eggs will scramble. Remove from the heat and stir in the cheese until it has melted into the custard. Pass through a fine sieve and leave to cool.

Pour the mixture into an ice-cream maker and freeze according to the manufacturer's instructions.

PG TIPS

Heat 100g sugar and 100g walnuts in a heavy based pan until the sugar dissolves, then raise the heat until it turns a rich gold. Pour into a lightly buttered baking tray and leave to go hard. Crush to a coarse texture, then add to the ice cream when it is almost finished in the machine. Remove and finish as normal.

I love cardamom as a spice, its fragrance working subtly within an ice cream base. This ice cream is delicious served with hot apple pie or pear *tarte tatin*.

cardamom
ice cream

50ml full fat milk
50ml double cream
2 tablespoon cardamom seeds,
 crushed
est of ½ orange
00g castor sugar
 egg yolks

Put the milk, double cream, cardamom seeds, orange zest and half the sugar in a saucepan and bring to the boil, then remove from the heat. Cream the egg yolks with the remaining sugar in a bowl, then pour on the hot cream mixture, stirring all the time. Pour this back into the pan and cook over a very low heat, stirring constantly with a wooden spoon, until the custard is thick enough to coat the back of the spoon. On no account let it boil.

When the custard has thickened, remove from the heat and strain, then leave to cool. Pour it into an ice-cream maker and freeze according to the manufacturer's instructions. If you don't have an ice-cream maker, follow the instructions on page 7 for making hand-beaten ice creams.

PG TIPS
For a tasty coffee variation, add 100ml of strong espresso coffee to the milk and cream.

sorbets

Originally buttermilk was the liquid left after extracting the churned butter from cream, known as traditional buttermilk. Cultured buttermilk is more readily available nowadays, made from lactic acid bacteria. This recipe balances the natural acid from the buttermilk and the lemon beautifully, rendering the sorbet light and creamy in texture.

buttermilk & lemon sorbet

250g castor sugar
250ml water
500ml buttermilk
juice and zest of 1 lemon
1 tablespoon honey

Put the sugar and water in a pan. Slowly bring to the boil, then remove from the heat. Pour into a bowl and chill in the fridge for 1 hour.

In a bowl, whisk together the buttermilk, lemon juice and zest and honey. Slowly add the syrup. Place in a sorbet or ice-cream machine and freeze according to the manufacturer's instructions.

PG TIPS
Add a dash of Italian *limoncello* liqueur to the sorbet base for an extra kick. Served with lemon tart or cheesecake, this is a real winner.

This recipe will be suitable for making sorbet with whichever your favourite berry is – simply replace the raspberries with your favourite variety. Mine is wild strawberries, of which I eagerly await the arrival in June or July.

raspberry sorbet

25ml water
150g castor sugar
150g fresh raspberries, hulled
and washed (frozen is fine)
100g icing sugar
juice of 1 lemon
1 tablespoon raspberry liqueur
(or sweet white wine), optional

Firstly prepare the sorbet syrup with the water and castor sugar, cook for 5 minutes, then allow to go cold. (This, like all sorbet syrups, can be made several days in advance and kept refrigerated.)

Place the raspberries and icing sugar in a bowl and leave to macerate for 30 minutes. Transfer to a blender and blitz to a smooth purée, then pass through a fine sieve to make a smoother sorbet.

Mix the purée with the cooled syrup, lemon juice and liqueur, if using, then place in the ice-cream machine and churn until it reaches a creamy sorbet consistency.

Transfer to a plastic container and cover with clingfilm or paper to prevent the formation of ice crystals within the sorbet. Top with the lid and freeze until required.

Mango sorbet is one of the loveliest and most refreshing sorbets to eat, served alone or with other exotic fruits on a hot summer's day. Make sure you choose mangoes that are firm but ripe in feel; if unripe they will be extremely fibrous and also tasteless. Indian mangoes are my favourite kind; I especially like the beautiful fragrances and perfume of the Alfonso variety.

mango sorbet

150g castor sugar
250ml water
450g mango pulp (taken from
  3 large mangoes, peeled and
  stoned)
juice of 1 lime

Prepare a classic sorbet syrup with the sugar and water: cook for 5 minutes, then remove and allow to go cold.

Place the mango pulp in a blender along with the lime juice and the cooled syrup, then strain through a fine sieve.

Transfer to an ice-cream machine and freeze according to the manufacturer's instructions, until a creamy sorbet consistency has been achieved.

Freeze in a plastic container, sealed over with a little clingfilm or paper, and cover with a lid. Freeze until required.

PG TIPS
Some chefs like to add 2 beaten egg whites to their sorbet, folded into the sorbet syrup prior to churning. This not only lightens it, but also helps extend the yield.

The distinctive tart-sweet flavour of passion fruit makes a wonderful tasting sorbet, the lime adding the perfect balance. I often serve it sitting proudly on a bed of diced mango and other exotic fruits, doused with a splash of tequila – why not?

passion fruit & lime sorbet

375g castor sugar
370ml water
juice of 2 limes
375g fresh passion fruit pulp
   and seeds

Put the sugar and water in a pan, slowly bring to the boil, then reduce the heat and simmer for 10 minutes or until the mixture becomes a thick syrup.

Allow to cool, add the lime juice and passion fruit and mix well. Place in a sorbet or ice-cream machine and freeze according to the manufacturer's instructions.

PG TIPS
For an unusual passion fruit salad dressing, mix together 6 tablespoons of the preparation with 4 tablespoons of vinaigrette. This works very well with prawn or lobster salad.

I think lychees are one of those exotic fruits that were made to be canned. They work much better than fresh in this particular sorbet.

lychee & lemongrass sorbet

2 tablespoons castor sugar
1 tablespoon finely grated
    fresh root ginger
4 lemongrass stalks, outer layers
    removed, tender inner core
    very finely chopped
100ml water
850g canned lychees
    in syrup
2 tablespoons white rum

Place the sugar, ginger and lemongrass in a pan with the water. Bring to the boil and simmer for 5 minutes, until the sugar has dissolved. Remove from the heat and leave to cool.

Drain the lychees, reserving 150ml of their syrup. Purée the lychees in a blender, then add the reserved lychee syrup and the lemongrass syrup and blitz to a smooth purée. Strain through a fine sieve into a bowl and stir in the rum. Pour into an ice-cream machine and freeze according to the manufacturer's instructions. If you don't have an ice-cream machine, follow the instructions on page 7.

is is a very good example of the way vegetables can give a
pecial flavour to desserts. I love this recipe: at the heart of
e icy coolness lurks the unmistakeable hint of hot chillies.

coconut milk, yogurt & red chilli sorbet

1 small hot red chilli
500g castor sugar
500ml water
400ml can of unsweetened coconut
    milk
250ml plain yogurt
4 tablespoons white rum

Cut the chilli in half lengthways, remove the seeds and dice very finely. Place in a pan with the sugar and water, bring to the boil and simmer for 1–1½ minutes or until the sugar has completely dissolved. Remove from the heat and stir in the coconut milk, yogurt and rum. Leave to cool.

Pour into a sorbetière and freeze until firm, following the manufacturer's instructions. If you don't have a sorbetière, pour the mixture into a bowl and place in the freezer. After 30 minutes, when the mixture is beginning to set, remove it from the freezer and beat well with an electric beater or hand blender to disperse any ice crystals, then return it to the freezer. Repeat this 2 or 3 times, then leave until the sorbet is set firm.

PG TIPS

In general, the smaller the chilli, the hotter it is. Always buy chillies that are firm to the touch. Once they become soft, they lose their fresh flavour.

Butternut squash and orange bring out the best in each other when combined in a simple recipe like this.

butternut squash & orange sorbet

500g castor sugar
500ml water
500g butternut squash, peeled and finely chopped
350ml fresh orange juice
5 tablespoons Grand Marnier (optional)

Bring the sugar and water to the boil and simmer for 1–1½ minutes or until the sugar has completely dissolved. Remove from the heat and set aside. Put the butternut squash and orange juice in a separate pan and cook until the squash is soft and pulpy. Transfer to a blender, add the sugar syrup and blitz to a smooth purée. Strain through a fine sieve and add the Grand Marnier, if using.

Pour into a sorbetière and freeze until firm, following the manufacturer's instructions. If you don't have a sorbetière, pour the mixture into a bowl and place in the freezer. After 30 minutes, when the mixture is beginning to set, remove it from the freezer and beat well with an electric beater or hand blender to disperse any ice crystals, then return it to the freezer. Repeat this 2 or 3 times, then leave until the sorbet is set firm.

PG TIPS
Replace the butternut squash with pumpkin and the orange with mandarin or clementine. All work wonderfully well.

This was the first cheese-inspired dessert I made when I began work on my *Passion for Cheese* book. For an interesting contrast, you could serve the rhubarb and punch syrup while they are still warm.

cream cheese sorbet

with rhubarb in chilled punch syrup

00ml milk
75g castor sugar
uice and zest of 1 small
  orange
75g cream cheese

**or the rhubarb in chilled
unch syrup**
50ml red wine
 tablespoons grenadine
  syrup
uice and zest of 1 orange
  cinnamon stick
5g castor sugar
50g rhubarb, peeled and cut
  into 5cm lengths

Put the milk, sugar, orange juice and zest in a pan and bring to the boil, stirring to dissolve the sugar, then remove from the heat and leave to cool. Stir this mixture into the cream cheese. Pour into an ice-cream maker and freeze until firm, following the manufacturer's instructions.

For the punch syrup, put the wine, grenadine syrup, orange juice and zest, cinnamon and sugar into a pan and boil until reduced by half its volume. Add the rhubarb to the syrup and cook gently for 5 minutes, until the rhubarb is tender and sweet but still holds its shape. Transfer to a bowl and leave to cool, then chill thoroughly.

Serve topped with scoops of the cheese sorbet.

PG TIPS

Make a *tutti frutti* style ice cream, by adding some finely chopped candied fruit and chopped nuts to the base. Choose a cream cheese that is fairly loose, not dry, in texture for the best results.

Whenever I taste this sorbet it immediately transports me back to a trip I made to the south of France near Cannes, where I first tasted something similar, served with a warm pear tart. I also like to serve it on a hot summer's day with a warm compote of orange and pink grapefruit delicately perfumed with a drizzle of Pernod in the syrup, simple yet inspiring!

fennel sorbet

300g castor sugar
400ml water
600g fennel (approximately 3–4 bulbs),
  roughly chopped
juice of 1 lemon
Pernod, to taste (optional)

Put the sugar and water in a pan, bring to the boil and simmer until the sugar has dissolved. Add the fennel, reserving some fronds for garnish, and poach gently for 10–15 minutes or until very soft. Pour into a liquidiser and blitz to a fine purée. Strain through a fine sieve and add the lemon juice and some Pernod, if using.

Pour into a sorbetière and freeze until firm, following the manufacturer's instructions.

PG TIPS
Serve a ball of fennel sorbet with gravadlax (marinaded salmon) or smoked salmon, to create a talking point at any dinner party.

This full-flavoured tomato sorbet makes an ideal appetiser on a hot summer's day. I like to serve it with fresh tuna *carpaccio* or prawns in a spicy, cocktail-style sauce, or just on its own. Make sure the tomatoes you buy are perfectly ripe.

roasted tomato & pineapple mint sorbet

1.5kg ripe plum tomatoes
250g icing sugar
125ml water
1 tablespoon lemon juice
a dash of Tabasco
1 tablespoon chopped fresh pineapple mint, plus a few leaves to decorate

Preheat the oven to 200°C/400°F/gas mark 6. Cut the tomatoes in half and remove the seeds. Place the tomatoes cut side down on a baking sheet and roast for 10–15 minutes, then transfer to a wire rack and leave to cool. When cool, peel them carefully and remove the central cores.

Put the icing sugar and water in a pan, bring to the boil and boil for 1 minute. Place the tomatoes in a blender, pour on the sugar syrup, then add the lemon juice, Tabasco and pineapple mint and blitz until smooth. Pour into a bowl and refrigerate until thoroughly chilled. Pour into a sorbetière and freeze until firm, following the manufacturer's instructions. If you don't have a sorbetière, follow the instructions on page 7 for hand beaten ice creams.

Serve decorated with pineapple mint leaves.

espresso granita

on *caffe latte* mousse

for the *granita*
75g castor sugar
200ml water
200ml strong espresso coffee
2 tablespoons Tia Maria or other
   coffee liqueur

for the *caffe latte* **mousse**
75g espresso coffee beans, finely
   ground
2 gelatine leaves
2 eggs
1 egg yolk
50g castor sugar
1 tablespoon Tia Maria or other
   coffee liqueur
225ml double cream, semi-
   whipped

to serve
100ml sweetened whipped cream
a few coffee beans

First make the *granita*. Put the sugar in a pan with the water and bring slowly to the boil. Simmer for 10 minutes, then add the espresso coffee and leave to cool. Add the coffee liqueur and pour the mixture into a shallow metal tray. Place in the freezer and, as it begins to freeze and ice crystals form, use a fork to scrape up the mixture from the sides and base occasionally, to flake the ice crystals.

For the *caffe latte* mousse, pour 175ml boiling water over the coffee and leave to infuse (ideally do this in a cafetière). Meanwhile, cover the gelatine leaves with cold water and leave to soak for 5 minutes. Drain well, squeezing out excess water. Strain the coffee, add the soaked gelatine and stir until dissolved. Leave to cool.

Put the eggs, egg yolk and sugar in a bowl set over a pan of simmering water, making sure the water is not touching the base of the bowl. Whisk with a hand-held beater until the mixture is creamy, pale and thick enough to leave a ribbon on the surface when trailed from the whisk. Remove the bowl from the pan of hot water, add the coffee liqueur and whisk until cool. Whisk in the coffee and gelatine mixture and leave until almost set, stirring occasionally. Finally, fold in the whipped cream and spoon into 4 large coffee cups or glasses. Place in the fridge until set.

To serve, top the *caffe latte* with a good spoonful of the *granita*, then with some whipped cream and coffee beans.

One of my favourite tipples before dinner (or at any time, if I am truthful!) is a good old G&T. In the summer, I like it with extra lemon and a sprig of mint, which funnily enough led me to think about a sorbet on the same lines. I tried it and here it is, served with thin slices of ripe pineapple.

gin, tonic & mint sorbet

with pineapple *carpaccio*

200g castor sugar
250ml water
1 good bunch of mint
300ml tonic water
100ml dry gin
juice of 6 lemons
grated zest of 1 lemon
1 ripe medium-sized pineapple,
 peel removed, thinly sliced

Place the sugar and water in a pan and bring to the boil slowly, to avoid the sugar crystallising. Remove from the heat and leave to cool, then add the mint (reserving a few leaves for decoration) and blitz in a blender. Strain and chill.

Combine the tonic water, gin, lemon juice and zest with the mint syrup. Pour into an ice-cream machine and freeze according to the manufacturer's instructions. (See page 7 if you don't have a machine).

Arrange the slices of pineapple on 4 serving plates, top with a scoop of the sorbet and decorate with the reserved mint.

A rich yet light chocolate sorbet is a great alternative to chocolate ice cream. Serve with a warm pear tart, or even as an accompaniment to a creamy Italian *tiramisù*.

chocolate sorbet

150g dark bittersweet chocolate couverture (70% solids) broken into pieces
500ml water
75g cocoa powder
250g castor sugar
60ml crème de cacao liqueur

Melt the chocolate in a bowl over a pan of simmering water.

In a pan, bring to the boil the water, cocoa powder and sugar to form a syrup. Cook for 15 minutes.

Stir in the melted chocolate and crème de cacao liqueur until smooth. Allow to go cold.

Transfer to an ice-cream machine and churn to a creamy sorbet consistency. Freeze in the normal manner, and use as required.

PG TIPS

For a marbled style chocolate sorbet, prepare the sorbet as for the recipe, then remove it from the machine and add 100g finely chopped white chocolate. Freeze as normal.

other frozen desserts

This black pepper parfait topped with a warm tomato, vodka and pineapple sauce is simple and inspiring. It makes a real dinner-party conversation piece.

black pepper yogurt semifreddo

3 organic or free-range eggs,
  separated
25g castor sugar
½ teaspoon vanilla extract
grated zest of 1 orange
150ml double cream
125g Greek-style yogurt
75g meringues, broken into pieces
1 teaspoon black peppercorns,
  lightly cracked

for the sauce
15g unsalted butter
1 tablespoon castor sugar
75g fresh pineapple, cut into
  5mm dice
2 firm, ripe tomatoes, peeled,
  deseeded and cut into 5mm dice
1 tablespoon vodka
juice of 1 orange

Put the egg yolks, sugar, vanilla and orange zest in a large bowl placed over a pan of gently simmering water. Whisk until the mixture doubles in volume and becomes pale and thick. Remove the bowl and leave to cool, whisking frequently to prevent a skin forming.

In 2 separate bowls, whisk the cream and egg whites until stiff. Add the yogurt to the thickened egg yolk mixture and then fold in the whipped cream, then the egg whites. Finally add the meringue and black pepper. Pour into ramekins and freeze overnight.

Dip the ramekins in hot water and run a knife round the edges to loosen. Turn out on to serving plates and defrost for 10 minutes while making the sauce.

Heat the butter, add the sugar and lightly caramelise. Add the pineapple and tomatoes, cook for 1 minute. Add the vodka and orange juice and boil for 1 minute. Pour the warm sauce over the semifreddo and serve.

Frozen yogurt ices are often seen as a healthier alternative to the traditionally made ice creams using fat, a craze I believe which first started in California. As one who does not worry too much about every calorie, I include a little optional cream to the recipe, which rounds the flavour.

frozen cherry yogurt

75g icing sugar
350ml good quality low-fat yogurt
juice of 1 lemon
300g fresh or tinned cherries in syrup, puréed (reserve a few for a garnish)
2 tablespoons kirsch liqueur
150ml whipping cream, semi-whipped
2 egg whites, beaten until stiff

Place the icing sugar and yogurt in a bowl and mix well. Add the lemon juice, puréed cherries and kirsch, then fold in the semi-whipped cream and beaten egg whites.

Transfer to an ice-cream machine and freeze until it begins to become thick and slushy in consistency. Transfer to a plastic container and freeze until ready for use. Take out about 20 minutes before serving to allow the yogurt to soften.

Decorate with fresh or tinned cherries.

PG TIPS

In summer, other fruits such as raspberries and strawberries are equally tasty prepared this way. In the autumn I plump for juicy blackberries.

iced lemon parfait

with *kadaifi* & warm cherry compote

for the iced lemon parfait
125g castor sugar
100ml water
zest and juice of 2 small
  lemons
5 egg yolks
200ml double cream, semi
  whipped

for the *kadaifi*
150 *kadaifi* (shredded wheat
  pastry – try Middle Eastern
  shops, or use filo pastry
  instead)
75g butter, melted
50g icing sugar, plus extra for
  dusting

for the cherry compote
450g black cherries, stoned
75g castor sugar
1 teaspoon lemon juice
1 teaspoon lemon zest
a little kirsch, to taste

sprigs of mint to decorate

Put the sugar, water and lemon zest in a pan, bring to the boil and cook until it reaches 110–115°C. Beat the egg yolks until they double in volume. Keeping the machine running, pour the hot syrup on to the yolks, add the lemon juice and continue whisking until the mixture is cold and quite aerated. Gently fold in the double cream. Pour the mixture into 4 ramekins (6cm), level the tops and freeze.

For the *kadaifi*, preheat the oven to 180°C/350°F/gas mark 4. Unwrap the dough and put it into a bowl, unravelling it slightly. Add the melted butter and icing sugar and gently work them through the dough with your fingers until it is well coated. Divide the *kadaifi* into 8 portions and shape them with a pastry cutter into rounds slightly wider than the parfaits. Place them on a baking sheet and bake for 8–10 minutes, until lightly golden, then leave to cool.

For the cherry compote, place 150g cherries in a liquidiser and blitz to a pulp. Strain, then transfer to a pan, add the sugar and 4 tablespoons of water and boil until the sugar has dissolved. Add remaining cherries and poach gently for 1–2 minutes. Stir in the lemon juice and zest and the kirsch.

Place a cooked *kadaifi* round on each serving plate. Turn out the lemon parfaits and place one on top of each, then top with the remaining *kadaifi* and dust with icing sugar. Pour the warm cherry compote around and decorate with mint.

Kulfi is an Indian-style ice cream preparation, especially rich and creamy in flavour but without the eggs used in an ice cream. Traditionally made in a variety of flavours with nuts and spices, it is utterly delicious. Here is my favourite *kulfi* recipe.

kulfi

125ml double cream
175ml full fat milk
½ teaspoon fresh or
   powdered saffron
½ teaspoon crushed
   cardamoms
2 tablespoon ground rice (or
   fine semolina)
30g castor sugar
225g evaporated milk
2 tablespoons finely chopped
   pistachios
2 tablespoons finely chopped
   almonds

to decorate
extra pistachios and sliced
   mango, to decorate

Heat the cream, full fat milk, saffron and crushed cardamoms in a pan and bring to the boil. Remove from the heat and leave to infuse for 10 minutes. Stir in the ground rice and sugar.

In another pan, bring the evaporated milk to the boil. Pour into the first pan, return to the heat and simmer for 5–8 minutes until the mixture thickens slightly. Remove from the heat and cool thoroughly, then strain through a fine sieve. Add the mixed nuts.

Transfer to a freezer-proof dish, cover and freeze for 1 hour until it begins to set. Using a spoon, mash up the cream to break up the ice crystals, then divide into individual *kulfi* conical moulds or ramekins, cover and freeze until required.

Serve, decorated with pistachios and fresh mango.

PG TIPS
Traditionally, kulfi is made in a mould and then turned out onto plates but it can also be served in a colourful bowl, as in the picture opposite.

iced walnut
semifreddo

with pomegranate syrup & pistachios

100g castor sugar
75g walnut halves
2 free-range eggs
75g white chocolate, melted
300ml double cream, semi-whipped to
  form soft peaks
1 quantity pomegranate caramel
  syrup (see page 93)
2 tablespoons roughly chopped
  shelled pistachios

Put 60g of the sugar in a heavy based pan over a low heat. Gently melt the sugar, then increase the heat until it cooks to a dark caramel-amber colour. Add the walnuts and cook for 30 seconds. Pour the mixture out into a tray and leave to cool, then finely chop it into small pieces.

Put the eggs and remaining sugar in a bowl and set the bowl over a pan of simmering water. Whisk until the mixture doubles in volume and becomes thick, dense and creamy. Remove the bowl from the heat and whisk it again until cool.

Add the melted chocolate, then fold in the semi-whipped cream and the caramelised sugared nuts. Pour into a clingfilm-lined terrine or individual moulds and place in the freezer overnight.

Remove the frozen semifreddo from the terrine or moulds. Cut the terrine into slices or, if using individual moulds, leave them whole. Pour over the pomegranate syrup, sprinkle with pistachios and serve.

A *cassata* is a chilled and moulded ice cream preparation, classically associated with Sicily. Here's a simple recipe I enjoy preparing.

cassata gelata

900ml prepared vanilla ice cream
  (see page 10)
100g crystallised fruits, chopped
30ml brandy
75g ricotta cheese
50g dark chocolate couverture,
  broken into small pieces
50g chopped peeled pistachios

to decorate
120ml whipping cream, semi
  whipped
25g peeled pistachio nuts

Place a 1.2 litre pudding basin or suitable bowl in the freezer to chill thoroughly.

Allow the vanilla ice cream to soften for 25 minutes in the fridge. Add the remaining ingredients to the ice cream and mix well. Line the pudding basin with clingfilm, allowing the excess to overlap over the edges of the basin.

Spoon the mixture into the basin. Ensure it is pushed down thoroughly into the base. Wrap over the overlapping clingfilm and secure it. Return to the freezer and freeze overnight.

To serve, remove from the freezer and turn out on to a serving dish. Leave to soften for 20 minutes before serving. Decorate with cream and pistachios and cut into wedges to serve.

iced ricotta parfait

with caramelised peppers

for the iced ricotta parfait
50g castor sugar
2 free-range eggs, separated
1 vanilla pod, split lengthways,
  seeds removed and reserved
250ml double cream
100g ricotta cheese
75ml Frangelico liqueur
zest of 1 lemon
hazelnut brittle (see PG TIPS) –
  optional

for the caramelised peppers
1 small red pepper, deseeded and
  cut into 1cm dice
1 yellow pepper, deseeded and
  cut into 1cm dice
4 tablespoons honey
1 teaspoon balsamic vinegar
juice of ½ lemon
50g soaked raisins, drained and
  dried
3 fresh tarragon leaves, chopped

Whisk together the sugar, egg yolks and vanilla seeds until pale and almost doubled in volume. Half whip the cream until soft peaks begin to form. In another bowl, whisk the egg whites until very stiff peaks form. Add the cheese, liqueur and lemon zest to the egg yolks and blend. Gently fold in the cream, then the egg whites. Spoon the mixture into ramekins. Cover with clingfilm and freeze for at least 3 hours.

Place the peppers in a small pan with the honey and lightly caramelise them for 3–4 minutes until soft and tender. Add the vinegar, lemon juice, raisins and tarragon and cook together for 5 minutes to form a light syrup. Remove from the heat and leave to cool. To serve, remove the parfaits from their moulds by quickly immersing them half way up in hot water, then turn them out on to individual serving plates. Leave to soften for 5 minutes. Pour the pepper syrup over the parfaits and serve immediately with the nut brittle, if desired.

PG TIPS

To make nut brittle, spread 50g chopped hazelnuts out on a lightly oiled oven tray. Dissolve 100g castor sugar in 2 tablespoons of water, bring to the boil and cook without stirring, until golden. Pour over the hazelnuts and leave to harden and go cold, then roughly crush the pieces.

caramelised cinnamon cassata

125g castor sugar
2 tablespoons freshly ground
  cinnamon
300ml full fat milk
300ml double cream
8 egg yolks
½ teaspoon vanilla extract
50g mixed almonds, walnuts and
  hazelnuts, lightly toasted and
  roughly chopped
40g mixed candied peel, finely
  chopped
½ teaspoon grated lemon zest
125ml sweet marsala

to serve
chocolate sauce (see page 84), lightly
  flavoured with marsala
amaretti biscuits

Put the sugar and cinnamon in a small, heavy based pan and heat gently until melted. Raise the heat and cook, without stirring, until it becomes a dark amber colour. Meanwhile, heat the milk and cream almost to boiling point. When the caramel is ready, whisk it into the cream mixture and set aside.

In a bowl, whisk the egg yolks and vanilla extract together. Carefully pour on the caramel cream mixture, whisking all the time, then return the mixture to a clean pan and cook, stirring, over a low heat until it has thickened enough to coat the back of the spoon. Remove from the heat and leave to cool. Churn in an ice-cream machine for 20 minutes until just beginning to set, adding the toasted nuts, candied peel, lemon zest and marsala just before the end of the churning process. Line the base of a 1.2 litre pudding basin or a 20cm springform cake tin with greaseproof paper, fill with the *cassata* mixture and freeze until required.

To serve, dip the basin or cake tin into hot water and then run a hot knife round the edge. Turn out the *cassata* on to a plate and cut into wedges. Serve with the chocolate sauce and some *amaretti* biscuits.

The art of making a bombe is layering the different ice creams from the outer shell to the centre. Use a 1.2 litre pudding basin if you can't find a bombe mould.

christmas bombe

600ml prepared vanilla ice cream
(see page 10)
50g candied pineapple, cut into
1cm cubes
50g candied lemon
25g dried sultanas, soaked until
plump
25g dried currants
50g glacé cherries, cut into small
cubes
50ml kirsch
600ml prepared pistachio ice cream

holly leaves, to decorate

Chill the bombe mould in the freezer overnight. Mix the vanilla ice cream with the fruit ingredients and kirsch. Remove the pistachio ice cream from the freezer and allow to soften slightly at room temperature for about 15 minutes.

Working quickly, spread an even 1cm thick layer of pistachio ice cream on the bottom and sides of the bombe. The best way is to use the back of the hand or a wooden spoon. Return to the freezer for 1 hour to set up firmly. When firm, fill the centre of the bombe with the vanilla fruit ice cream mix and smooth over the base of the bombe with a palette knife. Return to the freezer and freeze overnight or for at least 8 hours.

To serve, remove from the freezer approximately 30–45 minutes before serving to allow it to come to a suitable consistency. Hold a hot wet cloth around the bombe to loosen the outer surface. Lift off the mould and leave to soften. Decorate the bombe with holly leaves. Cut into wedges and serve. A chocolate sauce (see page 84) would accompany it beautifully.

sauces & accompanying dishes

If you start with good-quality chocolate, making a great-tasting chocolate sauce is a simple task. It's vital to use a chocolate with at least 60–70 per cent cocoa solids. This is the one thing to get right; after that, some cooks use water, some milk, some cream. All work well in their own way, and create sauces of different qualities.

chocolate sauce

250ml single or
   whipping cream
25g castor sugar
120g plain chocolate
   (60–70 per cent cocoa solids),
   broken into small pieces
25g unsalted butter

Put the cream and sugar in a heavy based pan and bring slowly to the boil. Immediately remove from the heat and, once off the heat, stir in the chocolate and butter until melted and smooth.

Serve warm or leave to cool.

variations
Add 2 tablespoons rum, Grand Marnier or another preferred liqueur to the finished sauce. Infuse the cream and sugar with 1 teaspoon ground ginger, then proceed as for the basic recipe. Alternatively, infuse the cream and sugar with 1 teaspoon lavender, rosemary or thyme leaves, and proceed for the basic recipe, but strain before cooling.

white chocolate sauce
Melt 200g white chocolate in a bowl over a pan of simmering water. Bring 250ml double cream and 4 tablespoons full fat milk to the boil, pour into the melted chocolate and add 10g unsalted butter. Stir with a wooden spoon until smooth. Add 1 tablespoon kirsch if desired.

My research leads me to believe that toffee sauce originated in Britain and the Scots added golden syrup to create butterscotch sauce. Either is wonderful poured over ice cream, or served with steamed sponge puddings.

toffee sauce

200g soft brown sugar
100ml double cream
100g unsalted butter
½ teaspoon vanilla extract

Put the sugar, cream and butter in a heavy based pan and cook gently over a low heat, stirring with a wooden spoon until the butter has melted and the sugar has dissolved. Increase the heat and bring to the boil, stirring constantly. Lower the heat again and simmer for 4–5 minutes.

Remove from the heat, stir in the vanilla, and serve warm.

butterscotch sauce

Adjust the quantities to use 75g sugar, 150ml double cream, 50g unsalted butter and 150g golden syrup. Make in the same way as the toffee sauce, but simmer for 8–10 minutes until the colour changes from a milky coffee to a rich caramel colour. Add 1 tablespoon Scotch whisky – or rum, brandy or Grand Marnier – along with the vanilla extract.

variations

Add 2 tablespoons crème fraîche to the finished butterscotch sauce to add a little tanginess. Alternatively, replace half the cream with coconut cream and use 50g rather than 150g golden syrup. Add ½ teaspoon ground ginger to the ingredients at the start of the recipe.

Coulis, made from puréed, strained fresh or frozen fruit, is one of the simplest of all dessert sauces to prepare. Fruit sauces add not only a fresh taste to desserts, but also a splash of colour and fragrance. They are traditionally served cold, but can also be served hot. Coulis is wonderful simply poured over ice creams and sorbets, or served with fruit tarts and puddings – a winner every time.

mango coulis

2 ripe mangoes, peeled and
cut into chunks
2 tablespoons icing sugar
1 tablespoon water
a few drops lemon juice,
to taste

Put the fruit in a blender with the icing sugar and water. Blitz for 20 seconds until smooth, then add the lemon juice. Adjust the sweetness with more icing sugar if necessary, then strain through a sieve and serve.

variations
Replace the mangoes with 225g raspberries and strawberries to make a red berry coulis. Alternatively, use 4 ripe nectarines or peaches, stones removed.

PG TIPS
Take care not to over-blend the fruits in a coulis, as it lightens the colour and removes their natural freshness. For fruits with a tarter flavour, such as redcurrants, add double the amount of sugar, bring to the boil and cool before serving.

Other citrus fruits, such as grapefruit, mandarins, oranges or limes, can be substituted for lemons in this sauce – you may need to vary the quantity of sugar according to the fruit and to taste. Add extra interest and complexity by infusing flavours of your choice - lemon verbena I've found very successful.

lemon sauce

grated zest and juice of 2 lemons
300ml water
60g castor sugar
15g arrowroot, mixed with
  2 tablespoons water

Put the lemon zest and juice in a heavy based pan along with water and sugar and bring to the boil. Whisk in the dissolved arrowroot and cook for 30 seconds, then strain through a fine sieve.

lemon curd sauce

225g castor sugar
120g unsalted butter
finely grated zest and juice of 3 large,
  unwaxed lemons
3 large free-range eggs, beaten

Put the sugar, butter and lemon zest and juice in a heavy based pan. Heat gently, stirring, until the sugar has dissolved and the butter has melted.

Add the eggs, stirring constantly over a low heat, until the curd thickens and leaves the sides of the pan clean. Remove from the heat and transfer to a jar. When cool, cover and refrigerate.

Sugar-based syrups are an easy way to prepare a simple yet delicious sauce. Pour them over ice cream, or drizzle over fruit salads or mousses.

flavoured syrup sauces

100ml water
200g castor sugar
100ml liquid glucose

Put the water, sugar and liquid glucose in a heavy based pan and stir with a wooden spoon until the sugar has dissolved. Heat the syrup and as soon as it reaches the boil, stop stirring and cook for 1 minute, until a lightly thickened syrup sauce forms. Remove from the heat, transfer to a bowl and leave to cool.

lavender syrup

Put 1 quantity of basic syrup and 1 teaspoon of lavender leaves into a pan and bring to the boil. Remove from the heat and leave to infuse for 30 minutes, then strain.

soft fruit syrup

Line a colander with muslin and place over a bowl. Add 225g soft fruit. Bring the basic syrup to the boil, then pour it over the fruits. Leave overnight to let the fruits release their juices. Stir in 1 tablespoon of fruit liqueur.

pomegranate caramel syrup

Bring the syrup to the boil with 1 tablespoon of pomegranate molasses. Allow to cool before adding 4 tablespoons of grenadine syrup. Try serving with iced walnut semifreddo (see page 72).

Mexico's famous caramel sauce is made from fresh goat's or sheep's milk, cooked down very slowly until it becomes a luscious, enriched, caramelised cream. It is traditionally served over ice cream, or as here drizzled over pancakes, which I love to combine with roasted bananas.

cajeta sauce

with vanilla pancakes & roasted bananas

for the *cajeta* sauce
750ml goat's (or sheep's) milk
75g granulated sugar
250ml whipping cream
1 fat stick cinnamon
50g chilled unsalted butter,
  cut into small pieces

for the pancakes
150g plain flour
1 tablespoon castor sugar
4 free-range eggs
1 teaspoon vanilla extract
150ml whipping cream
150ml full fat milk
vegetable oil, for frying

for the bananas
25g unsalted butter
4 bananas, peeled and halved
  lengthways
2 tablespoons icing sugar

For the *cajeta* sauce, put the milk, sugar, cream and cinnamon stick in a wide heavy based pan and bring it to the boil. Remove the cinnamon, lower the heat and simmer gently for about 2 hours. It will go through varying colour changes in this time, from light to dark caramel. Remove from the heat and whisk in the butter. Serve warm, or leave to cool. The sauce will keep in the fridge for 2 weeks.

For the pancakes, sift the flour into a bowl, stir in the sugar, and eggs and mix well. Add vanilla extract, cream and milk and leave to rest for 1 hour. Heat a little oil in a large frying pan. Ladle batter in small heaps around the pan and cook for about 1 minute until golden, then flip to cook other sides. Remove and keep warm.

Heat butter in another frying pan and add bananas. Dust with icing sugar and cook until caramelised.

Sandwich 2 banana halves between 2 pancakes on each plate, top with ice cream or yogurt and drizzle decoratively with *cajeta* sauce.

Take a few exotic fruits, vibrant with flavour and colour, combine with a scoop of home-made sorbet, and you have a refreshing fruit sundae.

tropical fruit sundae

with ricotta sorbet

for the sorbet
250g castor sugar
250ml water
600g ricotta cheese
2 tablespoons honey

for the sundae
1 mango, peeled and cut into
  1cm chunks
1 papaya, peeled, halved and
  seeds removed
2 kiwi fruits, peeled and cut into
  1cm chunks
1 banana, peeled and thickly
  sliced
125g strawberries, halved
juice and zest of 1 orange
1 tablespoon mint, roughly
  chopped
4 scoops of sorbet
150ml natural yogurt
2 passion fruits, halved
2 tablespoons flaked almonds,
  toasted

For the sorbet, put the sugar and water in a pan. Slowly bring to the boil, then remove from the heat. Pour into a bowl and chill in the fridge for 1 hour. Place the ricotta and honey in a food processor and slowly blend in the chilled syrup. Place in a sorbet or ice-cream machine and freeze according to the manufacturer's instructions.

Place all the fruits except the passion fruit in a bowl, add the orange juice, orange zest and mint and leave for 30 minutes in the fridge.

To serve, place a scoop of sorbet in 4 individual sundae-style glasses. Top with the fruits, then spoon over the yogurt. Scoop out the passion fruit pulp and seeds and drizzle over.

Sprinkle a few almonds over the yogurt and serve.

This refreshing dessert is packed with flavour and ideal for the summer months when nectarines are ripe, juicy and plentiful. Other flavours of ice cream would work equally well.

spiced nectarines

with vanilla ice cream

4 large firm but ripe nectarines
40g unsalted butter
10 black peppercorns, cracked
½ teaspoon Szechuan peppercorns
½ teaspoon dried pink peppercorns
½ teaspoon ground star anise
30g castor sugar
2 tablespoons kirsch

for the pistachio milk sauce
1 small tin condensed milk
30g peeled pistachios
1 tablespoon kirsch

4 scoops of vanilla ice cream (see page 10)

Preheat the oven to 230°C/450°F/gas mark 8. Cut the nectarines in half, twist and separate and remove the centre stones. To remove the skins, place in a pan of boiling water for about 4 minutes – the skins will start to wrinkle and fall off. Remove the skins and place the nectarine halves in an ovenproof baking dish.

Melt the butter in a non-stick frying pan, add the spices and cook for 1 minute. Add the sugar and 100ml water and lightly caramelise together; add the kirsch. Pour the syrup over the nectarines and place in the oven to roast for 5–6 minutes.

Meanwhile for the sauce, place the condensed milk, pistachios and kirsch in a food processor and blend until smooth.

To serve, pour a little pool of pistachio sauce in the centre of each serving plate or shallow bowl, add 2 nectarine halves, top with 1 scoop of ice cream and drizzle with the spicy syrup.

profiteroles

with white chocolate & basil ice cream

**for the white chocolate and basil
ice cream**
10 basil leaves
200ml double cream
200ml full fat milk
200g good-quality white chocolate,
  broken into small pieces
4 egg yolks
25g castor sugar

for the choux pastry
200ml full fat milk
65g unsalted butter, diced
20g castor sugar
125g plain flour
4 eggs
1 egg yolk, beaten with 2 tablespoons
  milk
2 tablespoons flaked almonds

hot chocolate sauce (see page 84)

For the ice cream, tear the basil leaves into small
pieces and set aside. Bring the stalks gently to the boil
with the cream and milk, and simmer for 1 minute.
Add the white chocolate, stir well, then remove from
the heat and leave to infuse for 10 minutes. Whisk
together the egg yolks and sugar until creamy. Strain
the basil-infused cream on to the egg yolks, whisking
constantly, then return to the pan and cook, stirring,
over a low heat, until the mixture thickens. Remove
from the heat and leave to cool. Stir in the torn basil
leaves, pour into an ice-cream machine and freeze
according to the manufacturer's instructions.

Preheat the oven to 200°C/400°F/gas mark 6. Put the
milk, butter and sugar in a medium pan and bring to
the boil. Quickly rain in the flour and beat with a
wooden spoon until the mixture leaves the sides of
the pan clean. Allow to cool slightly, then beat in the
eggs one by one to give a thick, glossy mixture. Place
walnut-sized mounds on to a lightly oiled baking sheet,
brush with a little of the beaten egg wash and sprinkle
over the flaked almonds. Place in the oven and bake for
15 minutes, then open the oven door slightly and leave
for a further 10 minutes. Remove from the oven, pierce
each profiterole with a skewer, then leave to cool.

Cut each profiterole in half horizontally, fill with a
ball of the ice cream and top with the lid. Arrange on
serving plates and pour over the hot chocolate sauce.

The colours in this dish are amazing: scarlet red pears in a contrasting syrup. A dish that is sure to impress, ideal for autumn and winter entertaining when pears are at their best.

pears in port & cranberry syrup

with buttermilk & lemon sorbet

4 large firm but ripe pears (William, or Comice varieties are ideal)
300ml cranberry juice
100ml port
100g castor sugar
zest of 1 orange
½ cinnamon stick
200g fresh or frozen cranberries
sprigs of mint, to garnish
buttermilk and lemon sorbet (see page 36) to serve

Using a potato peeler, peel the pears neatly, leaving the stalks intact and retaining the shape of the fruit. Cut a little off the base of each pear to help it remain upright during poaching.

Choose a saucepan that will hold the 4 pears upright side by side. Place the cranberry juice, port, sugar, orange zest and cinnamon in the pan and bring to the boil, stirring, until the sugar has dissolved. Add the pears, cover the pan and simmer for 20–25 minutes or until the pears are tender when pierced with a knife, but still retaining their shape.

Using a slotted spoon, remove the pears from the syrup and leave to cool. Add the cranberries to the syrup and boil rapidly until reduced by two thirds. Allow to cool, then pour over the pears and place in the fridge for up to 4 hours to chill thoroughly.

Garnish with mint and serve with the sorbet. Vanilla yogurt would make a good alternative.

gooseberry clafoutis

with black olive ice cream

for the black olive ice cream
100g black olives, stoned
100g sugar
250ml full fat milk
350ml whipping cream
6 free-range egg yolks

for the gooseberry clafoutis
2 free-range eggs
2 free-range egg yolks
80g caster sugar
30g cornflour
100ml full fat milk
200ml whipping cream
½ vanilla pod, seeds removed
and reserved
50g unsalted butter, melted
zest of ½ lemon
475g slightly underripe
gooseberries
a little icing sugar to dust

For the olive ice cream, cook the olives for 5 minutes in boiling water and then drain. Repeat this process 3 times to remove any bitterness, then chop finely. Put 50g sugar and 150ml water in a pan and slowly bring to the boil, raise the heat, add the chopped olives and cook for about 10 minutes until jam-like in consistency. Remove and set aside.

Preheat the oven to 180°C/350°F/gas mark 4. Heat the milk and cream in a pan with the candied olives until almost boiling point, then infuse over a low heat for 10 minutes. Beat the egg yolks and remaining sugar in a bowl until light and fluffy, then gradually whisk in the olive cream. Return to the pan, stirring constantly over a low heat until the mixture thickens enough to coat the back of a spoon. Remove from the heat, allow to cool, then freeze in an ice-cream machine.

For the gooseberry clafoutis, place the eggs, egg yolks and 30g sugar in a bowl and beat until light. Gradually add the cornflour and beat to a smooth batter. Add the milk, cream, vanilla seeds and 25g melted butter. Beat again until smooth. Put the remaining melted butter and sugar in a pan, add the gooseberries, lemon zest and 100ml water and cook for 8–10 minutes. Divide the gooseberries between 4 gratin-style dishes and then cover with the batter. Cook for 20–25 minutes until golden. Dust with icing sugar and serve with the black olive ice cream.

peach tarts

with buttermilk & lemon sorbet

for the tomato jam
600g very ripe tomatoes
120g icing sugar

for the pastry
250g plain flour
a pinch of salt
120g unsalted butter, diced
    (at room temperature)
25g icing sugar, sifted
1 free-range egg, beaten
1 free-range egg, beaten with
    1 tablespoon water, to glaze

4 white peaches
a little muscovado sugar
4 scoops of buttermilk & lemon
    sorbet (see page 36)
2 tablespoons flaked almonds,
    toasted

Blanch the tomatoes for 30 seconds, then peel, halve and remove the seeds. Chop very finely and place in a bowl. Stir in the sugar, cover and refrigerate overnight.

Sift the flour and salt on to a work surface making a well in the centre. Add the butter and sugar, then the beaten egg. Slowly bring the flour into the centre to make a dough. Knead very lightly for 1 minute, then form into a ball. Wrap in clingfilm and rest in the fridge for up to 1 hour. Preheat the oven to 200°C/400°F/gas mark 6. Roll out the pastry very thinly and cut out 4 12cm rounds. Place on a baking sheet, prick lightly with a fork, glaze with the beaten eggwash and bake until golden. Remove and leave to cool.

Drain the liquid from the tomatoes and simmer over a low heat until it is syrupy. Add the tomatoes and cook for 5 minutes, then remove from the heat and leave to cool. Spread the jam on to the pastry rounds.

Blanch the peaches for 1 minute, then remove with a slotted spoon and refresh in iced water. Peel, halve and remove the stones. Thinly slice each half. Arrange the slices on top of the tomato jam. Sprinkle each tart with sugar and grill until the sugar caramelises.

To serve, place a scoop of sorbet in the middle of each tart and sprinkle with the toasted almonds.

baked fruit kebabs

on chocolate couscous with fruit sorbet

for the couscous
200ml skimmed milk
1 teaspoon ground cinnamon
40g sugar
½ tablespoon cocoa powder
100g couscous
90ml rum (optional)

2 oranges
2 bananas
1 ripe pear
4 pitted prunes, soaked and halved
4 bamboo skewers, soaked in cold
   water for 30 minutes
4 tablespoons sugar
4 tablespoons water
2 tablespoons rum (optional)
fruit sorbet to serve

For the couscous, heat the milk, cinnamon and sugar in a small saucepan, add the cocoa, stir well and bring to the boil. Place the couscous in a bowl, pour over the chocolate milk, stir well, then cover and leave to stand for 5–8 minutes. Separate the grains with a fork, cover and leave for a further 5 minutes. Stir once again, add the rum, if using, and leave in the fridge.

Preheat the oven to 230°C/450°F/gas mark 8. Peel the oranges, bananas and pear. Cut each banana into 8 thick slices, cut the oranges into quarters. Halve the pear, remove the core, then cut into quarters. Thread the fruit on to the skewers, with the prune halves at each end of the skewers. Place the fruit skewers in a shallow ovenproof dish.

In a pan, boil the sugar and water for 5 minutes to make a syrup. Pour over the skewers, leaving a little aside for basting, and douse with rum, if using. Bake in the oven for 5 minutes, basting occasionally with syrup.

Serve the chilled couscous topped with the fruit kebabs, pouring over any remaining syrup. Serve with your preferred fruit sorbet, or with vanilla ice cream.

You may be amazed by this recipe – grilled figs in a vibrant green, spicy syrup that really adds zip to the fruit. A good dollop of vanilla ice cream completes an unusual dessert that never fails to impress.

coriander-lime grilled figs

with vanilla ice cream

1 bunch of coriander
juice from a 5cm piece of fresh root
  ginger
juice and grated zest of 2 limes
300ml Sauternes (or other sweet wine)
150ml glucose syrup
4 green cardamom pods, split
12 ripe purple figs
1½ teaspoons vanilla sugar (leave
  vanilla pods in a jar of sugar for a
  week to infuse the flavour)

Separate the coriander leaves from the stalks. Put the stal in a pan with the ginger juice, lime juice and zest, wine, glucose syrup and cardamom pods and bring gently to the boil. Reduce the heat and simmer for 5 minutes. Add the whole figs and poach gently for 3 minutes, then remove from the heat and leave to cool.

Remove the figs from the syrup and set aside. Return the syrup to the heat and simmer until it begins to thicken. Meanwhile, blanch the coriander leaves in a large pan of boiling water for a few seconds, then drain well and refres in iced water. Drain again and pat dry. Add the coriander leaves to the hot syrup and leave for 2–3 minutes. Pour th mixture into a blender and blitz until smooth. Strain and leave to cool, then chill.

Cut the figs lengthways in half and place on a baking tray Sprinkle with the vanilla sugar and place under a hot grill for 2–3 minutes, until caramelised. Arrange the figs on serving plates, add a scoop of ice cream, drizzle over the syrup and serve.

index

balsamic butter ice
cream 24
bananas, roasted 94
blackberry, frozen
yogurt 67
bombe, Christmas 80
buttermilk & lemon
sorbet 36, 103, 107
butternut squash &
orange sorbet 48
butterscotch sauce
87

cajeta sauce 94
caramel ice cream
22
cardamom ice
cream 33
cassata gelata 75
cheese sorbet 51
cherry
frozen yogurt 67
warm compote,
with iced lemon
parfait 68
chilli, coconut milk,
yogurt & red,
sorbet 47
chocolate
couscous 109
ice cream 12
mint ice cream 14
sauce 84
sorbet 60
white, & basil ice
cream 100
white, sauce 84
Christmas
bombe 80
pudding ice cream
10
cinnamon,
caramelised
cassata 79
citrus fruit salad 24
cloves 17
coconut
butterscotch sauce
87
coconut milk, yogurt

& red chilli sorbet 47
coffee
espresso granita on caffe
latte mousse 57
ice cream 33
cranberry 103

dried breadcrumb ice
cream 10

Earl Grey tea 10
egg nog & orange peel ice
cream 17

fennel
raisin and saffron ice
cream 18
sorbet 52
figs
grilled coriander-lime
110
freezing and storing ice
cream 7
fruit coulis 88
fruit kebabs 109

gin, tonic & mint sorbet
59
ginger chocolate sauce 84
goat's cheese ice cream
31
gooseberry clafoutis 104

hand-beaten method 7

ice-cream machines 7

kulfi 70

lavender 10, 84
syrup 93
lemon
curd 10, 90
iced parfait 68
sauce 90
lime
sorbet, passionfruit & 42
lychee & lemongrass
sorbet 44

mango
coulis 88
sorbet 40
mint chocolate ice
cream 14
nectarine
coulis 88
spiced 99
nut
brittle 76
ice cream 10

olive
black, ice cream 104
orange 17,
butternut squash &
sorbet 48

pancakes 94
parfait
iced lemon 68
iced ricotta 76
passion fruit & lime
sorbet 42
peach
coulis 88
tarts 107
pears in port &
cranberry syrup 103
pepper
black, ice cream 28
black, yogurt
semifreddo 64
peppers, caramelised 76
pomegranate caramel
syrup 93
profiteroles 100

raspberry
frozen yogurt 67
ice cream 27
sorbet 39
redcurrant coulis 88
rhubarb
in chilled punch syrup
51
rice pudding ice cream
10
ricotta 76
sorbet 96

semifreddo
black pepper yogurt 64
iced walnut 72
soft fruit syrup 93
strawberry
frozen yogurt 67
ice cream 27
sundae, tropical fruit 96
sweetcorn ice cream 21
syrup sauces 93

tea,
Earl Grey ice cream 10
toffee
ice cream 22
sauce 87
tomato
jam 107
roasted & pineapple
mint sorbet 54
vodka & pineapple
sauce 64
tutti frutti ice cream 51

vanilla ice cream 10

walnut semifreddo 72

yogurt 47
frozen cherry 67